LaTeasa R. Spears

Taking the Kingdom by Storm
One Godly Marriage at a Time

Cover Design By:
Jacquelyn Foster, Eden Creative Designs
EdenCreativeDesigns@gmail.com

Pearly Gates Publishing LLC
"Inspiring Christian Authors to BE Authors"
Pearly Gates Publishing LLC, Houston, Texas

Taking the Kingdom by Storm

Taking the Kingdom by Storm:
One Godly Marriage at a Time

Copyright © 2017
LaTeasa Spears

All Right Reserved.
No portion of this publication may be reproduced, stored in any electronic system, or transmitted in any form or by any means (electronic, mechanical, photocopy, recording, or otherwise) without written permission from the author or publisher. Brief quotations may be used in literary reviews.

ISBN 13: 978-1-945117-85-5
ISBN 10: 1-945117-85-0
Library of Congress Control Number: 2017950061

Scripture references are used with permission from Zondervan via Biblegateway.com.

For information and bulk ordering, contact:
Pearly Gates Publishing LLC
Angela R. Edwards, CEO
P.O. Box 62287
Houston, TX 77205
BestSeller@PearlyGatesPublishing.com

DEDICATION

I'd first like to start by saying this book has been a long time coming. I am so grateful to finally get it out into the world! I would not have been able to do this without the guidance of my Lord and Savior Jesus Christ. He's been with me every step of the way. When the journey got tough and I didn't think I would finish, He helped me get through it. With that being said, I dedicate this book to Him and the Kingdom of God!

To my children Phelicia, Malachi, Raphael, Ryleigh, and Trinity: You all bring me insurmountable joy! You all pushed me to keep going with every "I Love You!" I adore each one of you more than I could ever voice, and I want all of you to know Mommy loves you beyond this world!

I'd also like to dedicate this book to my parents, Mark and Krystal. As children, we pick up on so much from our parents — both good and bad. I want to thank both of you for the examples you set for us and for allowing us to make our own decisions. Both of you taught us a lot more than I'm sure you realize, and for that, I am grateful. I would not be the wife, mother, and woman I am without the life lessons both of you have showcased and allowed us to experience. I love you!

Last, but certainly not least, I'm dedicating this book to my husband, the love of my life, and my king: Rico. Babe, I can't even begin to explain how blessed I feel to have you as my husband! Every test and trial we've endured has brought us to this moment. I wouldn't change that for anything on this side of Heaven. You have stuck with me through thick and thin. You have taken our vows seriously and have taught me the true meaning of love and marriage. Thank you for sticking with me, even when you didn't want to. Thank you for listening to the voice of God, even when the stubborn part of you wanted to go your own way. Thank you for believing in me when I had not an ounce of confidence in myself. Jesus…I could go on and on. Just know: You mean the world and more to me! Here's to our eternal love! **I LOVE YOU INFINITELY!**

ACKNOWLEDGEMENTS

I feel like I cannot thank God enough for allowing me to be the vessel to deliver this book. This is a testament of His goodness, grace, mercy, and deliverance. He deserves ALL of the glory!

To Minister Catherine Storing: Thank you from the bottom of my heart for being my coach, teacher, and mentor throughout this book-writing process. Before encountering you, I never tried writing with the Holy Spirit as my guide. I have always written from a place of emotion. After being a part of your *Write Like A Pro* classes and incorporating the lessons God allowed you to convey, not only did it take me to higher heights with my writing, but also in my spiritual walk! That is how I know that meeting you was a part of God's divine purpose for my life! Thank you for all of your expertise and for having such an infectious, contagious, and loving spirit! You have been an integral part of this journey. That type of thing cannot be bought. You are priceless! I love you, Sis!

Taking the Kingdom by Storm

To Twila Favors: The fact that you are still here supporting and encouraging me after all of these years leaves me speechless. God took a nurse/patient relationship and turned it into a lifelong friendship and more. You have encouraged me—literally—from day one. I take great pleasure in having you in my life. Thank you for being my rock when I needed one. Thank you for your prayers. Most importantly, thank you for your love! You are next, my friend! I am believing God for it! I love you!

To my Best Friend, Denae Williams: The support I've received from you has been **REAL**! This journey that God has had us on for the past eight years has been nothing short of amazing! Your prayers and belief in me have been monumental, and I am so grateful to have you in my life. Thank you for being a listening ear late at night when I had no one else to talk to. Thank you for not judging me at *ANY* point in my life. Also, thank you for being willing to correct me when I'm wrong. That's what true friendship and sisterhood is about. You are the **BEST**! *Go, Best Friend!* LOL! I love you!

INTRODUCTION

I was asleep and happened to be dreaming about couples playing a newlywed game. They were talking about different topics, just as they do on the TV game show. The host asked questions about how they met, how they knew they were the one for each other, and even what made them decide to get married. The couples were blatantly honest. One couple even mentioned how the woman became pregnant, so they decided to get married and start their family.

I awoke from that dream and thought about how accurate that was for a lot of marriages these days. Shoot: My husband and I made an abrupt decision to get married…

We'd been engaged for two years and had our marriage license for months. The license was due to expire, so two days before its expiration, we decided to go ahead and get married.

I know. Crazy, right? I will explain the story behind our decision in the chapter to come.

Taking the Kingdom by Storm

I've seen and heard of so many marriages beginning as a knee-jerk reaction to something that happened. As stated previously, maybe the woman ends up pregnant; perhaps it was a rebound-relationship-turned-marriage based on a past relationship gone wrong; or a couple is relocating to another state and doesn't want to go as "just boyfriend and girlfriend", so they get married—just to name a few. The reasons are not all bad, but this tends to lead to issues in marriage because often times, one or both parties are not truly ready for the commitment. A lot of people see marriage as a quick fix for different issues in a relationship, but it's not that at all.

The reality is that marriage is hard work, and you have to be willing to make that investment. I say all of the time that *"A mother's work is never done"*. Truthfully, a **PARENT'S** work is never done—and neither is a spouse's, especially when you're a child of God. The enemy's goal is to kill, steal, and destroy. Even before you say "I Do", those are the enemy's motives. The covering that is necessary for marriage is one that you can never give up on and one that you have to set into the atmosphere daily. You can't marry just anyone and think that you'd be willing to make that crucial investment. Your heart won't be in it. You have to be willing to do anything for the person whom you come into covenant and Holy matrimony with.

I love seeing marriage occur between best friends! Yes: Your spouse **CAN** be your best friend and, in my opinion, he or she **SHOULD** be! I love seeing the plan come together that a couple has mapped out from the beginning. I love seeing the couples journey of being engaged all the way up to the wedding and the bliss that follows. It sort of makes a person believe in fairy tales!

Don't get me wrong: I **completely** understand that marriage is not all sunshine and rainbows. *However*, seeing a couple come together in a more "traditional" sense makes my heart so very happy! I'm not saying a marriage couldn't work under any other circumstance; I'm just saying the couple may be presented with more trials and tests if they're not quite ready. I know from firsthand experience. My husband and I faced a few mountains since saying "I Do", and I strongly feel they were a result of our getting married the way we did. Trying to build on an unstable foundation causes cracks and allows the enemy to seep through.

I want to help couples discover that ***"Aha! Moment"*** — you know…the moment when you know beyond a shadow of a doubt that he or she is **THE ONE** God sent to be your spouse. I'm not talking about the "Honeymoon Phase" where you're all lovey-dovey, everything is perfect, and you just *know* you want to be with that person for the rest of your life.

We all know the "Honeymoon Phase" passes and reality soon sets in. What I **AM** talking about is the moment after you've fasted and prayed for him or her, and you've had time to love on yourself enough to know your worth — so much so that when he or she comes along, they treat you no less than deserved because you won't allow it. Or even the moment when you've been with that person through thick and thin, and God has shown you that you had to go through those things to get closer to Him and prepare yourself for marriage.

The fact of the matter is this: **Everyone** deserves true and utter happiness in their marriage. If I can help at least one couple that is considering marriage to be patient, pray, and seek God about it before jumping in, then I will feel like I've done what I've set out to do with this book. The goal is not only to get married to your Heaven-sent mate, but to *STAY* married!

After each chapter, there is a journaling section. Write down your thoughts and feelings that were stirred up during your reading. Have fun with those!

I'll 'see' you on the other side!

TABLE OF CONTENTS

DEDICATION VI
ACKNOWLEDGEMENTS............... VIII
INTRODUCTION X
WHY THE RUSH? 1
TAKE YOUR TIME 13
ALL OF THE WRONG REASONS.... 21
LOVING ME FOR ME..................... 33
WHAT DOES GOD SAY?................ 45
DATING CAN BE FUN! 53
"AHA!" MOMENT 63
CONCLUSION 71
ABOUT THE AUTHOR 76

LaTeasa R. Spears

CHAPTER ONE

Why the Rush?

Marriage is the coming together of two individuals as one. The Bible says in Ephesians 5:31 (KJV), *"For this cause shall a man leave his father and mother, and shall be joined unto his wife, and they two shall be one flesh"*. Those two people are giving up the single life and all that it entails to share the rest of their lives with one another. So, why do so many people rush into marriage, knowing their "freedom" will be taken away?

I know there are a lot of different reasons, explanations, and/or excuses as to why. In my opinion, they tend to be a cover-up, need to justify something, or it's an opportunity to prove their love for one another to others. I can speak from personal experience on this.

I felt like getting married to my husband when I did would have changed our situation. I felt like saying "I Do" was going to make things better. So many people enter marriage with the mindset that things will get better or change once they say "I Do". But, is that really true?

Taking the Kingdom by Storm

Here's a little story about how things were for my husband and me before we said "I Do" and how I felt shortly afterward:

About two weeks before we got married, we had broken up. I had not been faithful to him, and he was over it. He felt as if he deserved better and sadly, I agreed with him. He didn't deserve to be treated in the manner in which I had treated him. I clearly showed him no respect and had no regard for our relationship in order to do what I had done. However, I also felt as though he was controlling, and I wanted to "live a little". I wanted to enjoy my life. I didn't need another father or person telling me what to do; hence, my rebellion towards him and our relationship.

One night, there was a knock at my door. He had walked over to my house (in the rain) after work. I was hesitant to let him in. I was in no mood to argue or play the 'Blame Game' with him. In the end, I chose to let him in.

We sat on the couch, talked, and then apologized to one another. We talked some more, apologized some more, and, by the end of the conversation some hours later, we decided we wanted to make things "right" and move forward with spending the rest of our lives together. We figured if we could make it through that recent episode, we could make it through anything. Plus, at that point, I felt like I had so much to prove to him. I felt like I was given a second chance to show both him and myself that I could be faithful and give my love to him…and only him.

I went online and searched for a licensed official who could marry us on that Saturday because if we'd gone to the Justice of the Peace, we couldn't marry on the day we wanted. We decided to tell only a few people and that everyone else would find out after we got married.

I told my parents, siblings, and two of my best friends. My future husband told no one about our upcoming nuptials…not his mother, not his sister, not even his best friend. At the time, that didn't stop my excitement. It was his choice and (at the time) I felt like he was doing it to protect me and also to prevent anyone from talking us out of marriage.

Taking the Kingdom by Storm

We had a lot to do in a matter of two days. We had two children whom we needed to have groomed and looking nice for the day. I needed my hair done and had to choose a dress. He needed his hair done (he had a head full of hair then) and had to find a suit. I'd already had a wedding gown, but I didn't want to wear that one yet since it wasn't the "big ceremony" we wanted. I figured I would save that dress for our vowel renewal.

Those two days flew by. My family was excited, but not everyone I told was able to attend. That was fine, considering it was short notice. I found a beautiful purple dress at Macy's. Purple is my favorite color, so I thought it was perfect! He wore a black suit with a purple shirt and very nice purple and blue tie. We dressed our beautiful babies to match accordingly.

The morning of, we were rushing and running around like chickens with their heads cut off. It was August and blazing hot that day. We were running late, and I was afraid the officiant would cancel on us for not being on time. We were getting married in the woman's home, so she could have surely canceled our appointment if she wanted to.

We all rushed to meet up at her house. I'll never forget riding in the car with my mother and my soon-to-be husband riding next to us yelling, **"MEET ME AT THE ALTAR! YEEEAAAHHH!"** as we drove down Riverside. We arrived at the officiant's home and entered. Her living room — the room in which we were to be married — was the same color as our attire. I mean, it matched *perfectly*! It was beautiful!

She had a full-body mirror in her small hallway. There was a beaded curtain that separated the hall and the living room. My father came, stood next to me, and said, *"Well, there's no aisle for me to walk you down. At least let me walk you into the next room. Just promise me that I'll still be able to walk you down the aisle at your big wedding!"* I said, **"*Of course, Dad!*"** My dad walked me into the next room and then Rico and I said our vows in front of God, our babies, and our six witnesses. We signed our marriage license — and we were now two become one!

Taking the Kingdom by Storm

I felt like the day we got married went perfectly, aside from being late to the officiant's house. We went out to eat, and would you believe? Our waitress' name was **DESTINY**! We ended up with a free meal. That night, as we were headed over a bridge with changing lights, by the time we drove over it, the lights were purple! I felt like that was a sign from the Lord!

However, wedded bliss didn't last two whole weeks…at least not for me. After almost two weeks of marriage, I found myself regretting my decision. I felt like I had made a mistake. Mind you: **NOTHING** had changed. We were still the same two people we were before "I Do". We had the same attitudes, the same tempers, and the same personal issues we had before—all still unaddressed.

Now, if I felt like that after only two weeks of marriage, it makes me wonder how long it takes for other couples who get married for all of the *wrong* reasons. The one thing I could say that I prided myself on was being faithful to my husband. Considering my past, that was hard for me—but I was doing it!

Coming from a broken home, there are things I remember from my childhood that I never want my children to experience. I have the ability to make sure they don't. I'd like to think that I am the generational curse-breaker in my family. That starts with my marriage.

Our marriage has been tested so much from day one. By the grace of God, we are still here. Even though we rushed into our marriage, God gave us the will to fight for it. Does that mean it's been an easy fight? Definitely not! Both of us have taken some gut-wrenching blows, but what kept us was our ability to get back up and fight harder.

I can't answer the question of why people tend to rush into marriage or why they don't take it seriously, but I do know that if they are not willing to fight for it, they might as well hold off on jumping the broom. The Lord says, "*The man who hates and divorces his wife does violence to the one he should protect*" (Malachi 2:16, NIV).

For some reason, the sanctity of marriage is now a mockery. It breaks my heart. Admittedly, I once helped make it that way. I've since learned from my mistakes and want others to as well. It's time to get some God-fearing couples in this world—ones who are ready to display how beautiful marriage truly is and can be. We need to show how blessed the unity of man and woman is in the eyes of God, especially when it's done in decency and in order.

LaTeasa R. Spears

Patience is a Virtue!

Do you think you're ready for the commitment of marriage OR would you be rushing into it at this point in your life? Explain your choice.

_____

_____

_____

_____

_____

_____

_____

_____

_____

_____

_____

Taking the Kingdom by Storm

LaTeasa R. Spears

CHAPTER TWO

Take Your Time

LaTeasa R. Spears

A lot of people enter into marriage and then when hard times arise, they are unsure of how to work out their problems. Divorce seems to be the easy way out, as opposed to fighting through their issues to reach a resolution.

I've heard it said so many times: "*Just let the courts resolve it.*" That is such a cop-out and often times unfair, especially to the person who deserves the most fairness in the situation. This mindset comes from couples not seeking Godly counsel before — or even during — marriage. It's so important before entering into this union that you have premarital counseling with an unbiased couple that will give you counsel straight from the Word of God.

My husband and I went to premarital counseling months before we got married. It wasn't easy. A lot of the time, I felt like I was being verbally attacked. I look back on it now and realize it was mostly because not only was I not ready for marriage, but I was wrong on so many levels when it came to our relationship. I didn't want our pastors to know the depth of my individual issues and taint the image of the person they knew as 'me'. I should have been most willing to share who I truly was with them in hopes that they would be willing to pray with and help me through my struggles. That is another reason I feel it's so important to work on **YOU** prior to marriage as well. (That will be discussed in a later chapter.)

Even though I felt the way I did during counseling, I would have done it over again — and actually finish it. Our pastors literally told us they firmly believed we were **NOT** quite ready for marriage…and boy, were they right! I think it's so funny how we can get some of the best advice, but not want to adhere to it because it was not necessarily what we wanted to hear. We asked them to be our counsel, yet went against the grain *and* their wisdom. Don't be like us. By the grace of God, we are still married and thriving. However, I feel as though my husband and I could have saved one another so much more heartache and trials had we stuck with our sessions and waited to say "I Do".

People frown on counseling and therapy like they're bad things. People tend to say things like, "*I don't need a Shrink!*" They tend to think they don't have any issues that need to be addressed and, if they did, they feel they could fix them all by themselves. The harsh reality is that most people need to be in some form of therapy. We all deal with individual 'issues'. Not all people's problems are along the lines of abuse, addiction, and so forth. But, if you have trust issues, talk to someone about them. If you were in the military or an accident and suffer from Post-Traumatic Stress Disorder, talk to someone about it. If you struggle with anxiety or depression, *please* talk to someone about it.

There are so many things that will surface after you marry someone, live with them day in and day out, and get to know them better. Both of you will need to depend on each other in ways you never imagined. So, why not do you and your future spouse a favor and talk to someone about things you deal with or suffer from internally on a daily basis?

Premarital counseling is not only important for you as a couple, but also for you as individuals. It's possible that some things could surface that will bring both of you closer than you were before. Sadly, there may even be some things that turn out to be deal-breakers. Wouldn't you rather know those things prior to walking down the aisle? Of course, you'd be hurt momentarily. However, that's where you find the positives in the situation. That would be a great time to thank and praise God for saving you from a doomed marriage.

I'm not saying premarital counseling will solve all of your issues beforehand, but it will certainly give your marriage a fighting chance. I believe it can bring clarity and a sense of certainty. Honestly, no one wants to have questions about their soon-to-be spouse's past. No one wants cold feet because they are simply unsure about their choice of mate. Let's be even more honest: Some people enter marriage still in love with another person, which sets their union up for failure before the rice is thrown.

I don't mean to paint any negative pictures here. I simply want you to understand how important it is to me that people enter into marriage with a sound mind and pure heart with nothing but the best intentions toward their significant other and, ultimately, themselves. I want to positively change people's outlook on marriage as a whole. I'd love to see marriages where divorce is not even an option as the couples seek the Lord in everything they do to keep their unions strong. Marriages like these still exist, and I want to be an inspiration to others to obtain and maintain this kind of union!

Your Happiness is Worth the Wait!

How important do you think it is to go to premarital counseling? Why?

_____

_____

_____

_____

_____

_____

_____

_____

_____

_____

_____

_____

_____

LaTeasa R. Spears

CHAPTER THREE

All of the Wrong Reasons

Okay… So, you've gotten married. You and your spouse have fallen on hard times. You are concerned that things will not work out, right? Maybe you feel like you've gotten married for all of the wrong reasons. What is the reasoning behind where you are now? Are the two of you experiencing issues due to lack of communication, infidelity, lack of trust, or a change in financial situation?

First, you must analyze why you are where you are. Has there been a change in the family dynamic (a new baby, separation, new job, etc.)? Has there been an issue with infidelity? Or, are you two simply not agreeing on important decisions in your lives? All of the aforementioned issues can put a strain on any marriage. The hard part is finding the root of the issue and confronting it head on with the best weapons possible: The Word of God and prayer.

The Bible says in 2 Timothy 2:15 (KJV), *"Study to shew thyself approved unto God, a workman that needeth not to be ashamed, rightly dividing the word of truth"*. Get yourself into the habit of reading the Good Book (Holy Bible) daily and see how much it helps you in your life. You will find ways to resolve issues that will give you a sense of peace in the end. 1 Thessalonians 5:17 (NIV) says, "Pray without ceasing". Take whatever qualms you may have to the altar, be consistent and diligent, and don't give up. Jesus **can** and **will** work things out for you!

It will take some time in order for things to be restored, but you must be willing to endure. You need to know that we serve a God whose words will not return void. So, be diligent in working to fix your marital problems. This will prove that you did not get married for all of the wrong reasons and that your intentions for your spouse and marriage are the best.

Something you need to make sure you stay away from is talking about your relationship with others. Sometimes, we think people have our best interest at heart, but they very well may not. Does that mean everyone wants to come against you or be negative? No, it doesn't. However, if you are not seeking Godly counsel from an unbiased source, it may be counterproductive.

We definitely have times when we want to vent. Please be mindful of those you choose to vent to. I know someone who is an amazing listener. His name is **JESUS**! Give *Him* a try. You will feel so much better after venting to Him. You can write down your feelings. You can sit quietly in a room and meditate. You can pray. Oh! Don't put a time-limit on your prayers. If you limit your time with Him, you may miss out on the very thing you are searching for: peace.

Trust me: God had a plan when He brought you and your spouse together in Holy matrimony. Anyone who knows me knows that I always say, "*Everything happens for a reason*". It's the God's honest truth! Sometimes, we never find out the reasoning behind why certain things occur, but one thing we can bank on is that there will be a reaction to it—good or bad.

The question now is: How do you get your marriage back on track and lined up with the will of God?

You begin by taking the first step: **PRAY!** A lot of people make the mistake of praying that their spouse changes. That should not be the prayer you are lifting up. The prayer should be for you to ultimately change for the better. Even if or when you feel like you're not doing anything wrong, pray that you can find different ways to show your spouse that you are there for them, no matter what. If there is something deeply-rooted in them that is making them stray away, pray that it be revealed in order for you to give them the support they need. Pray that you become the best spouse to cater to the needs of your spouse.

One thing is for sure—and two things for certain: You are their spouse, so only **YOU** can give the love they are searching for. They may sometimes think the grass is greener on the other side. If your spouse is thinking that, ask the Lord what you can do to satisfy them and keep them feeling that way. We have to know how to seek God in *EVERY* situation.

The power that comes with the covenant of marriage causes the enemy (the devil) to try absolutely **EVERYTHING** to tear it apart. But the Bible says in Matthew 10:9 (KJV), *"What God has joined together, let no man put asunder"*. Some of you may be thinking, ***"The devil isn't man"***. Guess what? You are right! **HOWEVER**, man (as in human) is just another distraction the enemy (the devil) will use to pull you away from your marriage.

I know. I've been down **THAT** road…

Yes, I once thought the grass was greener on the other side. I even went to water that grass in hopes that it wouldn't dry up and die. Instead, it turned brown and ugly. I looked back at my home and noticed the grass was all green, nice, and flourishing, so I wanted to go back. Did I feel stupid? Absolutely. Embarrassed? Sure. But God made me see my fault in it all and I prayed for a change…in myself.

After you've prayed for yourself and checked yourself on possible changes, **then** you pray for your spouse. Pray that they see your heart. Pray that they want reconciliation just as much as you do. Pray that you will fulfill their every need and that they will fill yours. Sometimes, the very things we feel we are missing or lacking are right there in our very own home. I found that out the hard way.

Believe it or not, it took me nearly six years into our marriage to get it right and to see where my fault lied. I never thought I wasn't wrong. As a matter-of-fact, I **KNEW** I was wrong. At some point, I even purposely tried to sabotage our marriage because I felt my husband deserved better and that I could not change. Isn't that crazy? I felt I was so deep in my dirt that I might as well do more in order to make my husband give up on me. Wow!!! The more I think about that, the more I realize how ridiculous my way of thinking was. It not only crushed him, it also caused me more pain than I could have imagined.

That is what we do with God. We feel like we are so deep in sin, we might as well keep going and digging a deeper ditch for ourselves, living the life we're living. At this point, we're too far gone, right? ***WRONG!*** The God we serve is such a loving and forgiving God, that if you repent and turn away from those worldly things, He will still love you unconditionally. He will give you a love that you never imagined you would be worthy of.

Believe it or not, He can do the same for your marriage. He did it for mine! Five and a half years into this thing, and I said, ***"No more! We are going to do this thing the right way. I am going*** *to give my absolute best ever to be the best wife I can be."* I told my husband, *"No matter what you do, I am going to show you that I am here for you. I am here for US!"* Galatians 6:9 (KJV) says, *"Let us not be weary in well doing; for in due season, we shall reap if we faint not".* We can make it because all things are possible through Christ!

Once I declared that over our marriage and gave my 100% effort, the outcome was overwhelming! We literally had our **BEST** year of marriage ever, and it was the first of many to come!

If you feel like you got married for all of the wrong reasons and that your marriage now is a reflection of that; if you feel like things are going down the drain, pray that the Lord opens your hearts and minds to the possibility of starting over with one another. Open up your hearts and minds to giving your absolute all to one another. It's **NEVER** too late for that. God grants us new grace and mercy every single day. Who are we to deny a second, third, or even fourth chance to our spouse?

Please understand: I am **NOT** in any way, shape, or form saying that you *HAVE* to stay with your spouse if they are cheating constantly, being abusive in any way, or anything of that nature. Please do not misunderstand where I am coming from. However, if my husband and I are a prime example of what it means to forgive, allow God to take over your marriage. If we didn't have the Lord as our foundation, we would be divorced. True story! Rico has stuck around through some of the worst times, and I honestly don't feel like I could have done the same if the shoe had been on the other foot.

I can say that we are still here—not only because I made a conscious effort to change, but also because my husband didn't give up, **EVEN** when he wanted to. He listened to the Lord and was obedient, **EVEN** when he wanted to chuck the deuces. I cannot thank my husband enough for his obedience. Without that, we would no longer be "us".

My husband showed me that even through his pain and all of the turmoil, listening to God and following His will for our marriage was far more important. The Bible says that His strength is made perfect in our weakness. God showed my husband the meaning of that for sure!

I am saying all of this to impress the following on you: **TRUST THE LORD!** Your marriage has a purpose! You both have a story that is unlike any other because it belongs to **YOU**! Use your journey for the glory of the Lord and to edify the Kingdom of God! He has great things in store for you. Your marriage is *NOT* null and void!

There is Purpose in Your Marriage!

What excites you most about God's ability to restore your marriage? Go into depth in your response.

_____

_____

_____

_____

_____

_____

_____

_____

_____

_____

_____

LaTeasa R. Spears

CHAPTER FOUR

Loving Me for Me

For some people, being single is rough. Most long for companionship, so being alone for too long is not ideal. This sometimes leads to unhealthy relationships just for the sake of being with someone. I was a person who was never alone, at least not long enough to get to know myself and discover who I was outside of a relationship.

For the first couple of years that Rico and I were together, it was on and off. This was mostly because I was conflicted in what I wanted and with the thought of settling down. Believe it or not, it was actually **ME** and *not* him. People have this perception that men are always the ones who do not want a commitment, but in our case, it was the other way around. I was confused because I didn't know what I deserved. I settled for less from others, which caused drama in our relationship.

My husband thinks outside of the box, so he's always wanted to give me the world and more. He's displayed this from the moment we began dating. For our first Valentine's Day, he took me to a five-star French restaurant and a play. Afterward, we went dancing in a private location. He made the night so special, and I truly enjoyed myself! However, I can honestly say I didn't know how to appreciate something like that. Am I saying I should have been reeled in because he wined and dined me? Absolutely not, but it was the thought and effort he put into the entire night that made it worthwhile. He wanted to make sure I knew I was special, and I felt that way! Now, that is a date I will **NEVER** forget!

That experience showed me that I was worth every bit of the treatment I received. Sadly, it took me years to actually feel like I deserved it. I had to get over my insecurities and low self-esteem. If I may be honest here *(which I've been doing all along)*: That's something I'm still working on, but God has brought me so far in my journey and I know I deserve to be treated like a Queen! My husband has always called me his 'Empress'. I thought that was something so special because I'd never heard that before—at least not addressed towards me.

As women, we need to understand that we are so much more than our outside appearance. We are so much more than our hairstyles, the clothes we wear, and the purses we carry. We are so much more than the cuddy-buddy *(and you know exactly what I mean)*. We are so much more than those "things"! It takes some true discipline to put sex on the back burner when it's something you've grown accustomed to. However, when you are determined to succeed and please God, you can do it!

We sometimes have to sacrifice the worldly things that we love so much in order to receive our blessings from God. We do that by being obedient to His Word.

"And Samuel said, 'Hath the Lord as great delight in burnt offerings and sacrifices, as in obeying the voice of the Lord? Behold, to obey is better than sacrifice, and to hearken than the fat of rams'"
(1 Samuel 15:22, KJV).

The blessing could come in the form of your future husband. Do not block your blessing because you're too selfish to sacrifice some worldly things. Give God the time and praise **HE** deserves!

You know what that obedience is called? I'll tell you: It's called fasting and prayer! Fasting and prayer work on a level you cannot begin to imagine. I've always heard that fasting worked, but I was not disciplined enough to actually complete a fast until recently, maybe in the past few years. You feel so much better, and God makes things clearer for you in that time. Often, you hear the phrase, *"Write it down and make it plain"*. That's what fasting and prayer do for you. God is going to make some things evident and plain for you. I have written down my prayers before and that has blessed me tremendously!

Isn't that ultimately what we all want? Clarity? I know I do! I don't want to go about life confused and misguided. I want to know that I'm doing things that will be pleasing to God and because I'm married with children, I have six other people to think about when I make decisions. Lord knows I hate making decisions, but it's a huge part of life…and there's no way around it. So, why not try to make the best decisions so that you're not making your life harder than it has to be? The saying goes, ***"Think smarter, not harder"***, right?

If your family consists of just you for the time being, make sure you seek God in all you do.

I'm telling you now, ladies: If you are spiritually-inclined and you know how to enjoy life, any man in his right mind would give anything to have you! The first thing that attracted me to my future spouse was the love that I saw he had for the Lord! The way he could use scripture to make me feel better and explain why he used said scripture showed me that he sought the Lord's guidance. He didn't just quote it and leave it at that. He broke it down and showed me how the Word of God was soothing and comforting. Think about it: Not every man/woman can do that! This is another reason you do **NOT** want to rush into marriage.

Just as God makes it plain to a man that he is supposed to marry you, He will make it plain to you that you're supposed to marry him. I knew that my husband was going to propose to me. Did I know how? Of course not…but I had a gut feeling that God had answered my prayers. We had a rough road leading up to our marriage (and even afterward for a bit), but I wouldn't change any of it. The experiences have brought us to a place where we could never be had we not gone through them.

Taking the Kingdom by Storm

Even though I wouldn't change anything, part of me can only wonder where we would be had we waited to get married. That definitely doesn't mean I wish we would have waited. Every argument and moment of discord brought us closer than I'd ever thought we'd be, and it taught us how to get along with one another — and how **NOT** to treat each other.

Okay. Let me stay on topic here.

Fellas, you can take some time to yourself as well. God will send the right woman for you. Just like you don't want women to think all men are the same, you need not think all women are the same. We definitely are not. We all bring different things to the table.

Believe it or not, before me, my husband had been celibate for three years. He says that it wasn't as hard as one would make it out to be. He literally focused on enjoying his youth and his life. He was in college and working a job where he made great money, so he focused on those things. He was able to find things that kept his mind off of sex. He then realized he didn't need sex to feel like he was a man. Personally, I feel like

God truly sustained him, and He can and will sustain you, too—if you are genuine in waiting for your wife.

There is purpose in everything we do. God has so much more in store than this world could ever give us. I believe at the end of each day, we all want to be able to say that God got the glory out of everything we did. If that's the case, we have to be willing to give up what we want in order to be the example God wants us to be for others. There's always someone watching us. What do we want them to witness?

One of my favorite songs by JJ Weeks Band says, "*Let them see You in me. Let them hear You when I speak. Let them feel You when I sing. Let them see You...Let them see You in me*". That is my prayer every single day—that people see HIM in every single thing that I do. I want my life to radiate Christ. Does that make me holier than thou? No, it doesn't. It makes me a servant of the Lord who is willing to die to myself daily in order to edify the Kingdom of God and ultimately give God the glory!

Taking the Kingdom by Storm

If you are waiting for the perfect person for you, wouldn't you want them to see the God in you? Not as a front; not just to get their attention, but to keep them and grow with them. You want to marry someone you can grow with spiritually. God will send that person to you when you are ready for them. Don't rush getting familiar with yourself just because you want someone to lie with at night. No one can love you better than you — other than God, anyway!

Ask yourself: Do I want to marry someone in the current condition I'm in? Honestly think about where you are in life right now. What can you bring to the table? How is your self-esteem? How confident are you in yourself? Where are you mentally? Where are you physically? How do you feel about other people's opinions of you? These questions are so important.

Once you are happy with the answers to those questions, then just *maybe* you're ready for a spouse. You may not have everything right (most people don't before they get married). Still...strive to be the best you can be for your future spouse. Give them many reasons to want no one but you. You will not regret taking the time to get to know yourself, and neither will they!

Taking the Kingdom by Storm

You Are Priceless!

Do you know your worth? If so, what made you realize it? If not, what's holding you back from finding out?

_____

_____

_____

_____

_____

_____

_____

_____

_____

_____

_____

LaTeasa R. Spears

CHAPTER FIVE

What Does God Say?

Throughout life's journey as Christians, we strive to be more like God. The road leading to marriage and thereafter is no different. We want to be as close to perfect as we can be. Before we truly decide we want to settle down, we hit some bumps in the road. However, once we have a made-up mind that we want to be married, we try to not mess up. We try to be the person our future spouse would love to have by their side, or at least we **should** be doing that.

One thing I see some people doing prior to marriage is strengthening their relationship with the Lord. I think that is amazing! That is something we ALL should be doing on a daily basis. Again, study to show yourself approved!

"Wisdom is the principal thing; therefore, get wisdom: and with all thy getting, get understanding."
(Proverbs 4:7, KJV)

Going into marriage, you want to be sure you're making a wise decision. The covenant of marriage carries too much weight, you have to be spiritually-equipped to tackle it.

Taking the Kingdom by Storm

I can honestly say that going into my marriage, I didn't spiritually-equip myself. That allowed for the enemy to come in and take over in more ways than one. The enemy knew what triggered me. He knew what could take my focus off of the Lord — and off of my husband. The only way he was able to do that was because I was not strong enough spiritually to recognize an attack of the enemy. I didn't have any sense of discernment. That lack led to adultery, trust issues, feeling like I was being controlled by my husband, and it even brought forth fear.

Yes: **FEAR**.

At one point, I was afraid of my husband and felt like he would harm me. All of this came about because not only did I fail to prepare myself coming into our marriage, I also failed to lift us up during our marriage. I didn't know how to. Thank God, though! One of us did! My husband knew how to pray us through tough times and hope for better.

It was hard for me to tell the difference between what God wanted for me and for our marriage, as opposed to what the enemy was throwing our way. This is the perfect example of why you should put on the whole armor of God prior to getting married. That prepares you a little bit more for the battle. We already know what the enemy is going to try to do and say. The Bible says that the enemy comes to steal, kill, and destroy. So, from day one, his plan is to destroy your union!

What does **GOD** say? How does **HE** say we are to handle things?

"And if one prevail against him, two shall withstand him; and a threefold cord is not quickly broken."
(Ecclesiastes 4:12, KJV)

God give us an outline to follow. It's similar to a syllabus in college: Before you even get fully into the course, your professor outlines your whole semester. Your professor lays out all expectations of you as the student and what you are to expect of him. The Bible is our syllabus. God tells us exactly how to go about marriage. For example, He tells us in Matthew 19:3-6 that a man is to leave his mother and father and cleave to his wife.

Taking the Kingdom by Storm

If we follow our outline/syllabus (Bible) in the way that our professor (Jesus) has spelled it out for us, we equip ourselves to pass the tests. God allows tests and trials to come our way. Think about Job. Job was an amazing servant of the Lord who can teach us all a great lesson on faith. That will be the very thing that gets you through the tough times; your faith in God. You have to know how to trust Him, even when it seems like everything is going wrong. Building your faith will help you so much while dating or on your journey to marriage.

Once you establish your foundation with God and build upon it, you have to be willing to wait on the Lord and what He has for you. The waiting part can be hard, but your end gain is definitely worth it. Knowing that God is sending you someone you can connect with spiritually to elevate one another to higher levels in Him is certainly worth waiting for...*at least I think it is.*

Another reason why it's so important to wait and see what God is saying is that you want to make sure you have someone who is not afraid to spiritually "go to bat" for you. You want to marry someone who can discern an attack of the enemy and cover you and your family.

As I stated before, the enemy used my weaknesses. Those things triggered me to his advantage. He was on his job to destroy our marriage—and me as a person. Had my husband not been spiritually-sound, there are a number of times when the enemy would have accomplished his task. With that, I am thankful to God for preparing my spouse. Even though I wasn't fully ready, he made sure Rico was! How amazing is that? He knows years in advance what will be necessary. What is there not to love about God?

Now, I ask you: **What does God say?**

If you are uncertain of what God is saying to you at this time, be still. The Bible says, "Be still, and know that I am God: I will be exalted among the heathen, I will be exalted in the earth" (Psalm 46:10, KJV). Just be patient and listen to that small, still voice. He will not steer you wrong. Honestly: Has He ever?

Taking the Kingdom by Storm

God Makes No Mistakes!

I want you to find some quiet time where you can meditate and focus on the Holy Spirit. Write down what God reveals to you in that moment.

_____

_____

_____

_____

_____

_____

_____

_____

_____

_____

_____

LaTeasa R. Spears

CHAPTER SIX

Dating Can Be Fun!

Many people think that when you're a Christian, you can't have fun and enjoy life. Don't even try to date because we all know what that leads to...right? **WRONG?** Being a Christian should not limit you in regards to dating in general. Of course, there are lines that are not to be crossed, but does that mean you can't have good clean fun?

That's what "courting" is all about; getting to know someone and establishing a relationship. Dating should be fun, spontaneous, and interpersonal. You are establishing a friendship — first and foremost — and getting to know this person you may grow to love. Being your spouse's best friend is important! You want to make sure you're the first person they run to if they are in need. That all begins with getting to know them during the dating process.

Now, let me tell you all something: I am not a guru when it comes to dating. It's just not my "area of expertise", but I do know that as a woman of virtue, there are certain things expected of you. I know that as a man of valor, there are certain things expected of you. I use the word 'valor' because it takes courage to get out and date. It takes nerve and bravery to sweep a woman off of her feet. That is not an easy task, especially with a 21-Century Woman. I'm just saying…! We are strong, confident, and independent women, so we need a man who can complement us and bring a lot to the table. We want that "WOW-factor" in our relationship!

Now, I could be wrong, but I would think that a man would want the same. You know…a woman who matches his "fly-factor", right? That's why it's important to get to know the person you're dating beyond the physical aspect. It's all well and good for you to be attracted to this person, but that's only going to last for so long once you find out that you and that person have nothing in common beyond physical attraction.

Not only that, but the Bible states we are not be unequally yoked with unbelievers. You want to be sure the person believes as you do. How far do you think the relationship would go if you had completely different spiritual views? It's something to think about…

Dating doesn't have to be this long, drawn-out process. There are some really fun things you can do that don't require getting sexually-involved in the end. One thing my husband and I like doing is going to comedy shows. We are not big on going to clubs—at all. In my opinion, they are traps. The drinking and dancing tend to lead to other things.

How about finding a concert in your area of an artist both of you may be interested in? Does your city have some kind of poetry event every month? How about a picnic? Some people think picnics are old-fashioned or corny.

Men: Fun Fact - *PICNICS ARE NOT CORNY!!!*

Women: *DON'T* bash a man for using his time, energy, and effort to plan a picnic for you!

Picnics are opportunities to have great conversations with your mate. Do a little bit of research beforehand to learn of the different things they like. Then, incorporate some of them into the picnic! Believe it or not, that is a gesture that leaves a lasting impression and gives your mate a beautiful memory (if all goes well...*LOL!*)

Taking the Kingdom by Storm

My husband (well, boyfriend at the time) set up a beautiful indoor picnic for me. It was candlelit and he had several of my favorite items sitting in the middle of the blanket. We talked, laughed, and shared poetry with one another! It was amazing!

Those are just a few random suggestions that immediately come to mind. Be creative! Women, sometimes men like to be surprised and also like to be shown they're not the only one who puts forth the effort when dating.

I did something grand for my husband last year, just to show him how much I love and appreciate him—and he said he will never forget it. It wasn't necessarily a 'date', but it **WAS** something unexpected. I threw him a surprise birthday party!

My husband was turning 30 and to me, it was a big deal. He'd told me about the fact that he hadn't had very many birthday parties as a child, and I wanted to show him that he was important and loved by many. I had three months to make the party happen, so I got started.

I was pregnant with our fifth (and final) child, but I was not going to let that stop me. I took to Pinterest for ideas. I went to Party City and Walmart to browse their party items. I slowly but surely bought items and hid them in the hatch of my van. Boy, was it hard making sure he didn't see all of the stuff! I found an amazing baker to design his cake. Last, but not least, I went on Facebook and invited some of his family and friends who were out of town. I also reached out to his boss and asked him to help me get some of his coworkers on board to attend the party!

I truly went above and beyond because I wanted to bring in my husband's 30th year of life in a grand way. His best friend and I set it up where they took the kids to the movies. Then, afterward, his friend lured him to the party. I was so nervous because I'd done so much to ensure everything went right. I was eight months pregnant, it was Spring (but hot outside), and I was worn out and tired. Still, I managed to pull it off! I was blessed to have help I didn't even expect to have in the end, which was amazing!

When my husband walked in, we all yelled **"SURPRISE!!!"** He went back out of the door then came back inside in disbelief. He was almost in tears *(I actually think he shed a few)*! I felt so accomplished in that moment because I'd tried so hard to make his party perfect for him. That was most certainly one of the proudest moments of my life, and it was all to please my spouse!

The dating process can be just as magical. You don't have to go all out by throwing surprise birthday parties (unless that's your heart's desire). However, do something that your significant other will remember for the rest of their life. Show them that you are listening to them. Show them that you care and want them to know just how much. This will make your journey through marriage less difficult.

I'm not saying if you go out and spend tons of money trying to make someone happy that it will take away all of their cares and worries. I **AM** saying you can lighten their load by being what they've been missing. Be the Godly love they have been longing for and show them there is nothing quite like it. I feel like that's what my husband and I have done for one another, and it started with that very first Valentine's Day date I mentioned earlier. He showed me how I should be treated, and I'll never forget it!

You're Worth the Date!

What's the most lavish, fancy date you can imagine being on? Now, do you feel like you're worth it? (I hope the answer is 'YES!') Why or why not?

LaTeasa R. Spears

CHAPTER SEVEN

"Aha!" Moment

I stated earlier in the book that I wanted to help you reach your "Aha!" Moment in your relationship. This is the moment we have all been waiting for! We have been longing to reach the moment when the lightbulb comes on in our heads and we say, *"This is it! He/She is the one I have been dreaming about! This is the person I have been praying for God to send me! This is the person I am going to **MARRY**!!!"*

If you are already there, how exciting is that? What exactly brought you to this moment? Was it the time you spent being single and getting to know yourself, then ultimately getting to know your significant other? Did your mate woo you and/or sweep you off of your feet and show you a Godly love unlike anything you've ever experienced before? (I sure hope so!) Or was it simply God saying, *"Son/Daughter, your moment has come. **THIS** is the person I've created just for you!"*?

The Lord knew what you needed and when you needed it. Some people rush the process, but we have to remember that **HIS** timing is perfect. He is *ALWAYS* on time! The song I remember from when I was younger says,

Taking the Kingdom by Storm

"He may not come when you want Him, but He'll be there right on time. He's an on-time God; yes, He is!"

Because He is such an on-time God, He knew how long you needed to be by yourself. He knew just what you needed to learn and how. He wanted you all to Himself so that you could understand how you are to be loved. Because His love is unconditional, we won't find another one like it. Of course, our prayer is that we find one as close to it as humanly possible. The Bible says husbands are to love their wives as Christ loved the church. We are the church, so this speaks of how Christ loves us! In the time you spent being single, He was preparing you to receive the love of Christ from your future spouse based on the way Christ **LOVES** you!

I knew when my husband was going to propose to me. I literally told a group of my friends that he was going to do it. I didn't know how or precisely when, but I had a strong gut feeling. That feeling was my "Aha!" Moment! It just seemed like everything aligned perfectly. I was anxious, nervous, and excited all at once. When August 1, 2008 came around, my dream came true! He proposed to me, and all I knew was he was perfect for me!

I can honestly say that even though my husband and I entered into our union the hard way (by not taking the advice of our pastors), now that we're here, I wouldn't have done it any other way. I knew in my heart from December 3, 2007 — the first time he told me he was in love with me — that he would be the man I married. I didn't know when we would reach the point of engagement or marriage, but I felt God had sent me my soulmate. We were definitely in the 'Honeymoon Phase' at that point, though. It took me nearly six years to get this married life right, but it doesn't have to take that long for you.

This is the moment you've been waiting for! Some of you may still be waiting, and that's okay. Don't go back to where you were or how you used to be because you're tired of being patient. Take this time to give God glory for keeping you until He sends your helpmeet.

The journey to that point is a rough one, with dating and getting to know and learn about someone; but the Bible says (and I'm

Taking the Kingdom by Storm

Take your time and let God do His thing! Let Him show you how important you are. Ladies, let God send your man to you! Proverbs 18:22 (KJV) says, *"He who finds a wife finds what is good and receives favor from the Lord"*. Be classy, but not stuck-up. Show him that you have morals and can keep yourself up. Men, when looking for your lady, do something that stimulates her mind and not her body. That in and of itself is a turn-on (if the woman has her head on straight). Just a heads-up: That does **NOT** mean "be pompous". *No one* likes that!

Learn how to pray for yourself and others. You are going to need that so much during your marriage. Learn to be grateful and thankful. We are blessed from the moment we open our eyes and take our first breath of the morning to the moment we doze off at night. Thank God for the person you have by your side to experience life with you!

Don't be against dating. You won't find your significant other by thinking all men or all women are the same. They are not. There are still great men and women out there who can meet your needs. If you have children, there is someone out there for you **and** your children. When my husband and I married, I already had my first daughter from a previous relationship as well as our son we had together.

Before getting married, do not be afraid to go to premarital counseling. If you're in premarital counseling, don't get discouraged or allow it to defeat you. It's all for a purpose: to enter into your union a better person. It will be you two against the world. Give your marriage a fighting chance!

If you are already married and facing problems, go to the Lord in heavy prayer. Show Him that you are not giving up on your marriage and show the enemy he can't take what God has given you. What God has for you is for **YOU**! Have faith that everything will work out. I learned that once I spoke *LIFE* into my marriage and refused to settle for less, that is what we received: **LIFE**! You will reap what you sow, right?

Another thing that brought about change in me was fasting. I truly feel like making the decision to fast and being disciplined enough to paraphrasing), "*The race is not given to the swift, nor the battle to the strong; but to the one that endures to the end*". You have endured some trials, my friend; but those are what get you to one of the most rewarding moments in your life! That is something to truly celebrate!

You are ready to become someone's spouse! That is a mind-blowing thing! If this is not your first marriage, that's okay, too. Hopefully, your soon-to-be spouse lights a fire in you that you have never experienced before. Being with your God-given love can and will do that for you!

Beloved, bask in the moment and understand that our Heavenly Father wants nothing but the very best for us. We need to do our part and believe that He will do His.

"For as the body without the spirit is dead, so faith without works is dead also."
(James 2:26, KJV)

The journey into marriage is not easy, but it's so worth it when the union is ordained by God. Be diligent and know that God is on your side.

REMEMBER:

*WHAT GOD JOINS TOGETHER, LET **NO MAN** PUT ASUNDER!*

You're THE One for Me!

What was your "*Aha! Moment*" experience like? If you've not had that experience yet, what do you imagine it will be like?

LaTeasa R. Spears

The topics discussed here are just the tip of the iceberg, but it is my prayer they have been helpful. I wanted to shed light on some things that should be considered prior to marriage—and even after the "I Dos" are said. I can only speak for myself and my experience *(there will be more to come from my husband in the future).*

Let's do a little recap of what's been discussed:

Marriage is something that people should approach with understanding, clarity, and sincerity. You must have an open mind and not expect it to go one way and one way only. I went into my marriage with such a negative mindset, and that trickled down into our relationship heavily. I'd like to see other couples experience less of the negativity and **MUCH** more of the love and joy that comes with marriage. The enemy is already going to come in and try to tear apart your union anyway. Don't give him the ammunition to do so! Put on the full armor of God so that you can take your stand against the devil's schemes *(see Ephesians 6:11)*!

follow through with it is what initially changed my marriage. God revealed things to me that I feel may not have been otherwise revealed. He can do the same for you, but you have to give Him the time to do so. Don't try to rush God's will.

I am prayerful that the points made here will help propel you to the next level. May God BLESS your union and be the foundation that holds it together, for without Him, everything falls apart. Let's put an end to all of the bad marriage statistics and replace them with successful marriages!

I love you all and want to see the best come from your marriages!

GOD BLESS!

LaTeasa R. Spears

ABOUT THE AUTHOR

LaTeasa R. Spears has always dreamed of being an author. Writing and helping others have been her passions since she was a little girl. While in high school, a life-changing event happened with her family, and it caused her to lose her desire to write. After graduating high school, she visited her grandfather for the first time and learned he was writing a book! That excited LaTeasa and, after reading his manuscript, ignited the fire within her to pick her pen back up and start writing again! Now, years later, God has removed her fear and doubt of going forward as an author—which then birthed *Taking the Kingdom by Storm: One Godly Marriage at a Time*!

LaTeasa is a woman of God and a loving and devoted wife to her husband, Rico. They have five amazing children and currently reside in Ohio. She and her husband are active in ministry and love speaking to and encouraging others…**TOGETHER**!

LaTeasa is a Co-Founder of Alpha Omega Iota Christian Sorority, Inc. (AOI) in Ohio, an organization that does outreach in the

Taking the Kingdom by Storm

community, mentors young ladies, and uplifts women who long for sisterhood.

If you would like more information or to contact LaTeasa and the women of AOI, please feel free to send a message to:
alphaomegaiota1@gmail.com.

If you would like to let LaTeasa know how Taking the Kingdom by Storm blessed you in any way, email her directly at:
authorlateasaspears@gmail.com!

LaTeasa R. Spears

www.ingramcontent.com/pod-product-compliance
Lightning Source LLC
Chambersburg PA
CBHW050507120526
44588CB00044B/1670